T0356615

GO, Dev!

Story by Rose Inserra
Illustrations by Eva Morales

Nelson

Go, Dev!

Text: Rose Inserra
Publishers: Tania Mazzeo and Eliza Webb
Series consultant: Amanda Sutera
  Hands on Heads Consulting
Editor: Gemma Smith
Project editor: Annabel Smith
Designer: Jess Kelly
Project designer: Danielle Maccarone
Illustrations: Eva Morales
Production controller: Renee Tome

NovaStar

Text © 2024 Cengage Learning Australia Pty Limited
Illustrations © 2024 Cengage Learning Australia Pty Limited

Copyright Notice
This Work is copyright. No part of this Work may be reproduced, stored
in a retrieval system, or transmitted in any form or by any means
without prior written permission of the Publisher. Except as permitted
under the *Copyright Act 1968*, for example any fair dealing for the
purposes of private study, research, criticism or review, subject to
certain limitations. These limitations include: Restricting the copying to
maximum of one chapter or 10% of this book, whichever is greater;
Providing an appropriate notice and warning with the copies of the
Work disseminated; Taking all reasonable steps to limit access to these
copies to people authorised to receive these copies; Ensuring you hold
the appropriate Licences issued by the Copyright Agency Limited ("CAL"
supply a remuneration notice to CAL and pay any required fees.

ISBN 978 0 17 033397 9

Cengage Learning Australia
Level 5, 80 Dorcas Street
Southbank VIC 3006 Australia
Phone: 1300 790 853
Email: aust.nelsonprimary@cengage.com

For learning solutions, visit **cengage.com.au**

Printed in China by 1010 Printing International Ltd
1 2 3 4 5 6 7 28 27 26 25 24

*Nelson acknowledges the Traditional Owners and Custodians
of the lands of all First Nations Peoples. We pay respect
to Elders past and present, and extend that respect to
all First Nations Peoples today.*

Contents

Chapter 1

Dev's Big Secret

Dev and Will were back at school for the final term. It was a hot and sticky day.

"It's no fun at school when it's so hot," said Dev, as they arrived at their classroom.

"I know," said Will, fanning himself. "I'd love to be back at Ruffey's Beach camping ground right now. I wish you had come to visit me there over the holidays."

"Umm ... sorry. I wanted to come, but we were busy," replied Dev.

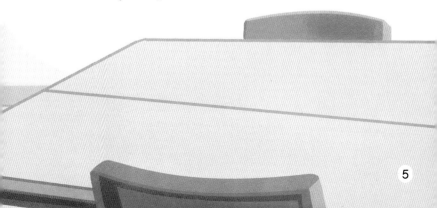

Dev didn't want to lie to Will. But he couldn't tell his friend the real reason he didn't go to the beach.

Inside the classroom, Miss Georgios had a special announcement.

"I have exciting news," she said, with a grin. "Our end-of-year picnic will be at Ruffey's Beach!"

Dev's classmates cheered. But Dev was quiet. He had only been at his new school since last term. He hadn't told his friends his big secret – that he couldn't swim.

Dev remembered the time when he was little and had visited his grandparents. They had taken Dev to the local waterfall. He had been so excited that he had run straight into the water.

His grandad had rushed in after him, but Dev had gone too far in.

The cold water had rushed into his nose and mouth. He had tried to take big gulps of air, but he felt like he couldn't breathe.

Dev remembered feeling relieved when his grandad had pulled him out of the water.

Since then, Dev had avoided going in the water. And now he still couldn't swim.

Dev's mum and dad had tried to take him to swimming lessons, but he hadn't wanted to go.

Maybe it's too late to learn to swim before the beach picnic, thought Dev.

Chapter 2

The Secret Is Out

After school, Dev and Will went to soccer training.

"We're going back to Ruffey's Beach camping ground over the summer," said Will. "Why don't you come and visit? We can swim and look for fish."

Dev looked worried. He didn't know how to tell Will his secret.

"Will, I ..." he began to say, and then stopped. What if Will laughed at him?

"I'll ask my mum and dad if they can take me," Dev said, hoping Will would forget and not ask him again.

The next morning at school, Will met Dev at the gate.

"Did you ask your parents about coming to Ruffey's Beach?" asked Will.

Dev decided it was time to tell Will his secret. He took a deep breath.
"Will, I ... can't ... swim," Dev said.

Will opened his mouth in surprise.
Dev waited.

"That's okay, Dev," replied Will in a gentle voice.

Dev took another deep breath, relieved. Will hadn't laughed at him at all.

"Hey, what if I come with you to the swim school at the pool in town? I can swim in the lane next to you," Will suggested.

Swimming lessons would be more fun with Will at the pool, too, thought Dev.

"Okay. Let's do it!" said Dev.

Chapter 3

The Shallow End

At the first swimming lesson, Dev was scared to go in the water. His swimming teacher, Sandy, gave him a pool noodle.

Then, Dev walked into the pool at the shallow end.

Dev looked at Will in the big pool next to him. Will waved. Dev waved back.

Sandy taught Dev how to breathe out in the water by blowing bubbles.

At the second lesson, Dev wore goggles so he could see underwater.

At the third lesson, Sandy gave Dev a kickboard to hold onto. Now he could kick his legs behind him and move forward in the water.

At the fourth lesson, Dev used the kickboard to practise without Sandy's help.

All this time, Will was in the next pool, cheering Dev on. Will and Dev even stayed back after each lesson to keep practising.

"I got you a present," said Will, on the last day of Dev's lessons.

"Flippers!" said Dev. "Wow! Thanks!"

Chapter 4

Ruffey's Beach

On the day of the school picnic, Dev was nervous. The water at Ruffey's Beach wasn't calm like the swimming pool. What if it was too deep? What if he went under the water?

Will and his classmates raced from the picnic spot to the shore.

"Are you ready, Dev?" Will shouted.

Dev followed Will and slowly dipped his feet in the water. It was cool and clear. He walked into the water until it was up to his hips. Then, he went all the way in until he was finally swimming.

Will splashed alongside Dev and gave him a high five. "Good job, Dev!" said Will. "I knew you could do it."

"Thanks," said Dev. "I couldn't have done this without you."

"Now you can come to our camping ground over the holidays," said Will. "Do you know how to fish?"

Dev grinned. "No, but I'm good at learning!" he said.